✴ HISTORY STARTING POINTS ✴

HATSHEPSUT
and the
ANCIENT
EGYPTIANS

DAVID GILL

W

Franklin Watts

Published in Great Britain in paperback in 2018
by The Watts Publishing Group

Copyright © The Watts Publishing Group 2016

Series editor: Julia Bird
Editor: Sarah Silver
Series designer: Matt Lilly
Picture researcher: Diana Morris

ISBN 978 1 4451 6207 2

FSC
www.fsc.org
MIX
Paper from
responsible sources
FSC® C104740

Printed in China

Franklin Watts
An imprint of
Hachette Children's Group
Part of The Watts Publishing Group
Carmelite House
50 Victoria Embankment
London EC4Y 0DZ

An Hachette UK Company

www.hachette.co.uk
www.franklinwatts.co.uk

Picture credits: AFP/Getty Images: 29. Konstantin Aksenov/Shutterstock:
11. Taras Boyko/Dreamstime: 16t. Patryk Cosmider/Shutterstock: 24. Dennis
Cox/Alamy: back cover. cybercrisi/Shutterstock: 15tl. De Agostini/Getty
Images: 21t, 21b, 30t. Design Pics Inc/Alamy: 15b. Ecophoto/Dreamstime:
15tr. Ecoprint/Shutterstock: 15cr. Werner Forman Archive: 2c, 26b, 28.
Dieter Hawlan/Dreamstime: 18b. Jim Henderson/Alamy: 17t. Peter Horree/
Alamy: 16b. incamerastock/Alamy: front cover b. Anton Ivanov/Shutterstock:
front cover, 12b. Peter Langer/Superstock: 13b. Metropolitan Museum NY/
Alamy: 25b. Metropolitan Museum NY/Wikimedia: 1, 2t, 4t, 22, 23tl, 23tr,
27, 30b. Jaroslav Moravcik/Dreamstime: 4b. mountainpix/Shutterstock: 14l,
25t. Naypong/Shutterstock: 15cl. Perseomedusa/Alamy: 13c. Dario Lo Presti/
Shutterstock: 13t. Science & Society PL/Getty Images: 20t. Fedor Selivanov/
Shutterstock: 18t. Przemyslaw Skibinski/Shutterstock: 8b. Jose I Soto/
Dreamstime: 19t. Tenback/Dreamstime: 4-5 bg. Serge Vero/Shutterstock:
17b. Wikimedia commons:2b, 9, 10t, 19b. WitR/Shutterstock: 10b. World
History Archive/Alamy: 26. Wrangel/Dreamstime: 23b.
Mikhail Zahranichny/Shutterstock: 12t.

Contents

MEET HATSHEPSUT

Hatshepsut ruled ancient Egypt from around 1479 to 1458 BCE. Although she was a successful female ruler, she vanished from Egyptian history after her death. Almost 3,000 years later, archaeologists and historians have managed to piece together her story.

This statue of Hatshepsut is on display at the Metropolitan Museum in New York, USA.

Who was Hatshepsut?

Hatshepsut was a member of the royal family of Egypt. She was the daughter of the **pharaoh** known as Thutmose I (also spelt Tuthmosis) and his chief wife, Ahmose.

When did Hatshepsut live?

Hatshepsut was born around 1504 BCE, 1,000 years after the pyramids were built, during the period in ancient Egyptian history now known as the New Kingdom. She was the fifth pharaoh of the 18th **Dynasty**, the same family dynasty as Tutankhamun, although he lived 120 years later.

Pharaoh Tutankhamun died when he was 17. The beautiful objects discovered in his tomb have made him famous.

4

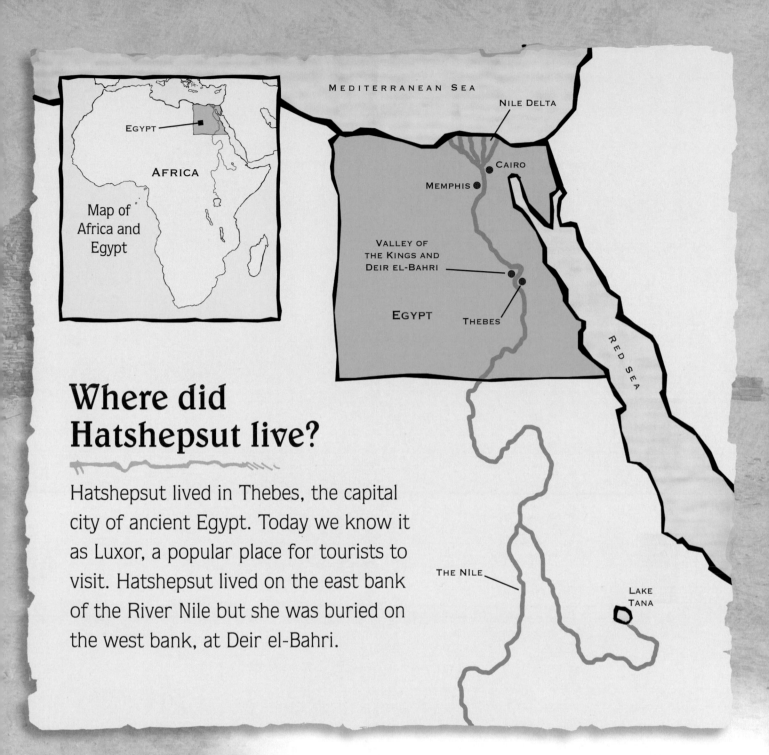

MEDITERRANEAN SEA

NILE DELTA

AFRICA

EGYPT

Map of
Africa and
Egypt

CAIRO

MEMPHIS

VALLEY OF
THE KINGS AND
DEIR el-BAHRI

EGYPT

THEBES

RED SEA

THE NILE

LAKE
TANA

Where did Hatshepsut live?

Hatshepsut lived in Thebes, the capital city of ancient Egypt. Today we know it as Luxor, a popular place for tourists to visit. Hatshepsut lived on the east bank of the River Nile but she was buried on the west bank, at Deir el-Bahri.

Why is Hatshepsut famous?

Hatshepsut was a great and powerful female ruler of ancient Egypt at a time when it was unusual for women to hold power. In addition, someone tried to destroy all records of her reign, including statues of her as pharaoh, after her death. Both of these facts have made many people fascinated by Hatshepsut.

HATSHEPSUT'S LIFE STORY

The story of ancient Egypt has fascinated people all through history with its strange beliefs, its haunting images and mysterious writing. Just as curious and fascinating is the story of Hatshepsut.

1

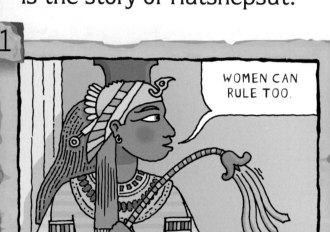

WOMEN CAN RULE TOO.

HATSHEPSUT WAS THE GREAT GRANDDAUGHTER OF AHMOSE-NEFERTARI, A STRONG LEADER AND MUCH LOVED QUEEN.

2

BEFORE BECOMING PHARAOH, HATSHEPSUT'S FATHER WAS A FAMOUS GENERAL WHO LIKED HUNTING, WHEN HE WASN'T FIGHTING EGYPT'S ENEMIES.

3

HATSHEPSUT MARRIED HER HALF-BROTHER, THUTMOSE II, WHEN SHE WAS ABOUT 13 YEARS OLD. THEY HAD A DAUGHTER.

4

YOU ARE NOT OLD ENOUGH TO BE PHARAOH.

WHEN THUTMOSE II DIED, HATSHEPSUT RULED IN HIS PLACE AS HER STEPSON, THUTMOSE III, WAS TOO YOUNG TO TAKE CHARGE.

5

As soon as Hatshepsut came to power she gave orders for a temple and **TOMB** to be built, where she would be buried.

6

Hatshepsut led her army to fight their old enemy, the Nubians, who lived to the south of Egypt.

7

Throughout her reign, Hatshepsut had a close relationship with her chief advisor, Senenmut.

8

During Hatshepsut's reign many people in Egypt became richer through increased trade with other countries.

9

NOW NO ONE WILL REMEMBER HER!

After her death statues of Hatshepsut were vandalised as if someone wanted to erase her memory.

10

Finding Hatshepsut's body was a mystery that archaeologists tried to solve for hundreds of years.

BUT WHICH ONE IS HATSHEPSUT?

THE RIVER NILE

Without the River Nile, the ancient Egyptians could not have lived in Egypt. Egypt has the biggest and hottest desert in the world so it was important to have a water source to feed all its people.

Source of the Nile

LAKE TANA

BLUE NILE

WHITE NILE

LAKE VICTORIA

Rivers all have a source, a starting point, usually somewhere in a hill or mountain. At Khartoum in Sudan two large rivers flow into each other. One is called the Blue Nile and its source is Lake Tana in Ethiopia. The other is called the White Nile and its source is Lake Victoria in Uganda. Together they form the River Nile, the longest river in the world.

FASCINATING FACTS

THE NAME NILE COMES FROM THE GREEK 'NEILOS', WHICH MEANS RIVER VALLEY.

Lake Victoria and its falls were named after Queen Victoria in 1855.

8

Climate change

Six thousand years ago, the land that is Egypt was grassland, with large lakes, and animals such as giraffes and hippos. Over time, climate change made North Africa hotter and drier. By the time Hatshepsut lived, much of the land was desert. Today, the Sahara Desert covers most of Egypt.

My own research

Climate change has happened several times in the Earth's long history. Recent records show that the average temperature of the Earth is increasing. Use library books and the Internet to find out what effects the increase in temperature will have on different places around the world.

An ancient Egyptian wall painting showing people harvesting reeds called papyrus. Papyrus was used to make boats and paper.

The best soil

Although ancient Egypt was mostly desert, farmers grew all kinds of food. This was because almost every year the river flooded the land nearby and left behind black silt, which was very good for growing crops.

THE AGE OF PYRAMIDS

A thousand years before the reign of Hatshepsut, pharaohs built pyramids that pointed up to the stars and to Ra, the great sun god. Over 130 pyramids were built across Egypt.

Five firsts

1. According to tradition, a man named Narmer became the first ever pharaoh around 3100 BCE.

2. Egypt became the first ever nation when Narmer united Upper and Lower Egypt.

3. The first pharaohs were buried in deep pits at Abydos, north of Thebes.

The Narmer Palette dates from about 3200 BCE. It is throught to show Narmer killing his enemy and uniting Upper and Lower Egypt.

People travelled great distances to see the amazing Step Pyramid from as early as 2000 BCE. Some of these visitors even left some graffiti behind!

4. The first capital of Egypt was Memphis, near the mouth of the Nile Delta.

5. King Djoser was the first pharaoh to build a pyramid, around 2650 BCE. It is called the Step Pyramid because it has six layers or steps, providing a 'stairway to heaven'.

A resting place

Each pyramid was designed to house the **mummified** body of a pharaoh. A passage was built inside the pyramid. The Egyptians believed this allowed the dead pharaoh to ascend into the heavens and that each night the pharaoh would sail across the sky with Ra, the great sun god. By the time of Hatshepsut, Egyptian rulers were building magnificent stone tombs rather than pyramids.

The Great Pyramid of Giza

The Great Pyramid of Giza is the only one of the **Seven Wonders of the World** that can still be seen today. It lies on the edge of Cairo, the capital city of modern Egypt. The Great Pyramid is made up of 2.3 million blocks of stone. It took an army of people just under thirty years to build.

The Great Pyramid of Giza

FASCINATING FACTS

PYRAMIDS WOULD HAVE LOOKED VERY DIFFERENT TO THE WAY THEY LOOK TODAY. THEY WERE FINISHED WITH A HIGHLY POLISHED WHITE **LIMESTONE** AND GOLD TIP THAT WOULD HAVE REFLECTED THE SUN'S RAYS AND MADE THE WHOLE STRUCTURE LOOK DAZZLINGLY BRIGHT!

LIFE AND DEATH

The people of Egypt, especially pharaohs, spent lots of time, money and energy preparing for the afterlife.

From death to life

For Hatshepsut, death was a doorway to the afterlife, where she'd be for eternity with the gods and goddesses. Like all pharaohs before her, Hatshepsut began preparing for her death as soon as she came to power. She ordered that a magnificent **mortuary temple** be built in her honour. Her body would be buried deep into the cliff behind the temple, at the end of a series of secret tunnels and chambers.

Hatshepsut built a huge mortuary temple at Deir el-Bahri near the Valley of the Kings.

Mummification

A mummified body now in a museum

All ancient Egyptians believed that they needed to preserve their body after death so that it could still act as 'home' for their soul. Mummification was a way of preserving the body's soft tissue. Internal organs such as the stomach, lungs and liver were removed and placed in **canopic jars**. The heart was replaced inside the body, once the body had been dried out by layers of salt. Finally, the body was wrapped in strips of linen. The whole process took about 70 days.

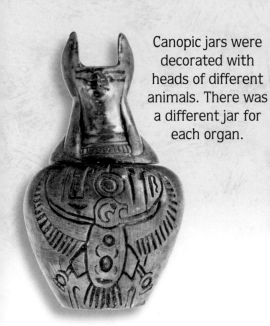

Canopic jars were decorated with heads of different animals. There was a different jar for each organ.

My own research

Salt absorbs water and it is used to dry things out. Try sprinkling salt on a piece of cucumber or tomato and watch what happens.

Weighing the heart

People believed that before they entered the next world they would travel on a journey filled with all sorts of dangers. Finally, they would enter the Judgement Hall where their heart would be weighed by Anubis, Guardian of the Scales. If their heart was weighed down by evil and wrong doing then they would be fed to Ammit, a fearsome creature made up of different animals.

An Egyptian wall painting shows the weighing of the heart, with Anubis on the left.

HISTORY LINKS

MUMMIFICATION WASN'T ONLY PRACTISED BY THE ANCIENT EGYPTIANS. THE CHINCHORRO COMMUNITIES IN NORTHERN CHILE AND SOUTHERN PERU CAREFULLY PRESERVED THEIR DEAD FROM AROUND 6000 BCE, THOUSANDS OF YEARS BEFORE THE EGYPTIANS.

A Chinchorro mummy of a baby

EGYPTIAN GODS AND GODDESSES

Anubis, god of embalming

The Egyptians believed in many gods and godesses. Each one was connected to a part of life, from birth to death. Some were local to a town or village but most were worshipped across Egypt and were shown on the walls of temples and tombs.

Sekhmet, with the face of a lioness, was the goddess of war because lions were fierce, aggressive creatures.

Gods from the animal world

Egyptians painted pictures of their gods and goddesses on the walls of temples and tombs. When imagining how they might appear, Egyptians drew inspiration from the animals around them. By Hatshepsut's time gods and goddesses had begun to look more like humans. It can be tricky to identify some of them as the same god and goddesses can be portrayed in different ways.

Keeping the gods happy

Egyptians believed it was vital to please the gods and goddesses and keep them on their side. Priests and rulers worshipped them by performing ceremonies in temples, while ordinary people worshipped gods and goddesses in their own homes.

My own research

Look at these pictures of animals that lived in ancient Egypt.

Use library books or the Internet to find out the names of the gods or goddesses these animals represented.

Can you find out what their role was?

The letters of their names are jumbled up here to help you:

cow

hippo

crocodile

falcon

bekos, throah, ttwerae, urhos

Answers on page 32

Amun: king of the gods

At the time of Hatshepsut, the god Amun became the most important god. He was the god Hatshepsut worshipped more than any other and she built many monuments to honour him. On the walls of her temple, Hatshepsut told the story of how she became the child of Amun. This was Hatshepsut's way of telling everyone how important she was, daughter of the king of all gods.

Amun was sometimes drawn with a ram's head and sometimes with a human face. He wore a double crown of tall feathers.

KARNAK

The ancient Egyptians believed that temples were the homes of gods and goddesses. The Karnak temple complex was dedicated to Amun, king of gods.

The temple complex

The Karnak temple complex was built at Thebes. All pharaohs during that period, including Hatshepsut, built a new temple, chapel or **obelisk** inside Karnak to honour the god Amun. It became the largest temple complex in the world.

The Karnak temple complex

Colourful images

Senenmut, a close friend and advisor to Hatshepsut, was given the job of organising all the building work at Karnak. Throughout the complex, statues of gods and goddesses, pharaohs and important people were built. The walls and columns of the buildings at Karnak would have been covered with colourful images of pharaohs, stories of the time and people making offerings to the gods. Senenmut also designed Hatshepsut's mortuary temple (see page 12).

A statue of Senenmut from Karnak

Hatshepsut at Karnak

Hatshepsut had five obelisks built at Karnak but only one is left standing there today. The biggest was 30 m high and was the tallest building in the world for hundreds of years. Hatshepsut also built the famous Red Chapel at Karnak. Inside was the sacred statue of Amun, the god who Hatshepsut said was her father. No other pharaoh had ever tried to link themselves so closely to one of the gods.

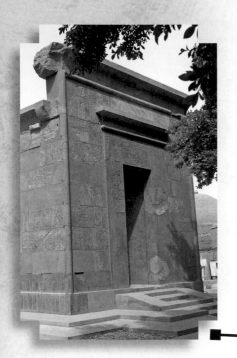

Red Chapel

Chief Priest

As pharaoh, Hatshepsut was given the role of Chief Priest. She would have been the only person Egyptians thought able to communicate with Amun. Hatshepsut often performed ceremonies at the Red Chapel. She would have presented offerings of food, water and animal sacrifices to the statue of Amun. Incense was burned to give a sweet fragrance to please Amun.

Cleopatra's Needle in London was actually made during the reign of Hatshepsut's stepson, Thutmose III.

HISTORY LINKS

THE CITIES OF LONDON, PARIS AND NEW YORK EACH HAVE AN EGYPTIAN OBELISK. ALL THREE ARE KNOWN AS CLEOPATRA'S NEEDLE BUT THEY ARE NOTHING TO DO WITH CLEOPATRA. IN FACT, THEY WERE ALL MADE OVER A THOUSAND YEARS BEFORE HER LIFETIME. THE OBELISK IN LONDON WAS GIVEN TO BRITAIN BY EGYPT AFTER THE BRITISH FOUGHT **NAPOLEON'S** FORCES IN EGYPT, IN 1815.

HIEROGLYPHS

Ancient Egyptian writing is called hieroglyphs. The word means 'sacred carvings'. We know a lot about Hatshepsut and other pharaohs from hieroglyphs.

Pictures and symbols

Hieroglyphs are pictures and signs of people, animals and everyday objects that represent a word or a sound. They can be written top to bottom, or across the page, left to right, or right to left. If the symbol is facing left then you read from the left.

FASCINATING FACTS

FOR HUNDREDS OF YEARS NO ONE COULD UNLOCK THE MEANING OF HIEROGLYPHS. IN 1822, A FRENCH SCHOLAR CALLED JEAN-FRANÇOIS CHAMPOLLION HAD A BREAKTHROUGH WHEN HE REALISED THAT WRITINGS ON THE ROSETTA STONE WERE WRITTEN IN ANCIENT GREEK, HIEROGLYPHS AND DEMOTIC.

The Rosetta Stone was found in Egypt by French soldiers of Napoleon, in 1799.

Scribes

The very first piece of writing found in ancient Egypt dates back to about 3250 BCE. It shows men using simple pictures to represent money that had to be paid to the pharaoh. The men writing them down were called scribes. Scribes had to study for a long time to use hieroglyphs as there were over 700 different signs for them to remember! Scribes used hieroglyphs to illustrate stories on the walls of tombs and temples.

Most Egyptians couldn't read or write so being a scribe was an important job.

Charcoal ink

Scribes wrote on papyrus, made from papyrus reeds that grew by the River Nile. Strips of the reeds were placed on top of each other and then pounded together until they resembled paper. The scribes wrote with a black ink that was made by burning wood to create charcoal and then diluting it with water. Gums or resins found in plants were used to bind the mixture together and make it stick.

Things to do

Important Egyptians had their name carved into a special stone name-plate, called a **cartouche**. Use the website below to find out how your name can be written using hieroglyphs and then make your own cartouche.

www.childrensuniversity.manchester.ac.uk/learning-activities/history/ancient-egypt/writing-in-hieroglyphs/

Hatshepsut's cartouche shows her as the daughter of the god Amun.

EXPEDITION TO PUNT

Hatshepsut heard stories about an exotic land to the south where there were strange creatures and valuable goods to buy. She sent a trading expedition down the Red Sea to seek out this mysterious land the Egyptians called Punt.

Kit boats

Five boats were sent out by Hatshepsut. The boats would almost certainly have been carried over land which meant they would have been built in kit form and put together when they reached water. The boats

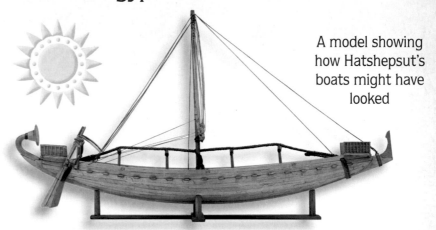

A model showing how Hatshepsut's boats might have looked

were approximately 20 m long and 5 m wide in the centre. Oars and sails were used to power the boat.

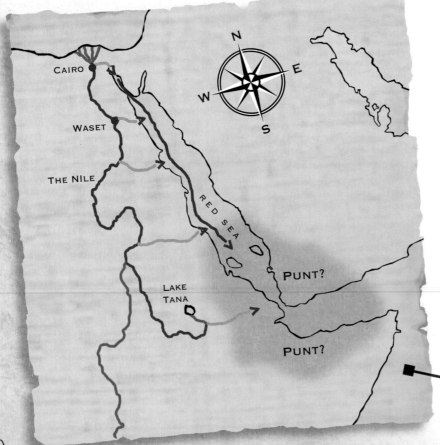

CAIRO

WASET

THE NILE

RED SEA

PUNT?

LAKE TANA

PUNT?

Map showing likely routes to Punt

The route

No one knows the exact location of the land of Punt. Historians believe it was part of the country now called Somalia. A likely route for the expedition would have been to sail down the River Nile towards Cairo and then turn east and on to the Red Sea.

THE DAILY EGYPTIAN

THREE CHEERS FOR QUEEN HATSHEPSUT!

The expedition to Punt has safely returned laden with wonderful gifts for our glorious queen.

Since the boats were spotted two days ago people have lined the banks of the Nile to welcome them home.

Let us not forget those who doubted the wisdom of sending such an expedition. Some said it was too dangerous and others simply did not believe a place called Punt existed. 'It was a fantasy,' they said but today such people must eat their words for the ships have returned with great quantities of **myrrh**, **frankincense**, ivory and creatures not seen before in Egypt.

May the name of Hatshepsut be remembered through eternity for this wonderful triumph.

Growing rich from trade

Sending an expedition across the sea to an unknown land was risky because if it had failed Hatshepsut would have been blamed. But it was a great success. We know from pictures drawn on Hatshepsut's mortuary temple that the expedition brought back gold, elephant tusks, panther skins and live monkeys. Hatshepsut opened up other trade routes with nearby countries that brought wealth for traders and glory for herself.

Thirty-one living frankincense trees were brought back from Punt and planted outside Hatshepsut's temple at Deir el-Bahri.

CREATING THE RIGHT IMAGE

Hatshepsut stands out from the many Egyptian women who held power because she dared to call herself pharaoh, King of Egypt.

Pharaoh, not regent

Many women had held great power in Egypt by ruling in place of a male heir who was considered too young. Such women were known as **regents**. As soon as the boy was old enough to rule, he usually replaced his mother or stepmother and became pharaoh. But Hatshepsut began to call herself pharaoh, and no longer behaved as a regent. Her stepson had to wait until Hatshepsut died before he became King Thutmose III.

 ## Image of a perfect pharaoh

Hatshepsut knew that if she was to have the authority of a pharaoh people had to accept her as ruler of Egypt. Hatshepsut did four things to convince people that she was the right person for the job.

1. She built lots of temples and monuments to please the gods and the Egyptian people.

2. She declared herself to be the daughter of Amun, king of all gods.

3. She took over the religious duties performed by the pharaoh at ceremonies in temples.

4. She created the perfect image of a strong Egyptian pharaoh.

This sphinx sculpture shows Hatshepsut with the powerful body of a lion and a man's beard.

A female king

At the start of her reign images of Hatshepsut made her look like a woman. But gradually, these images changed to make her look more like a man because people were used to men being the pharaoh. They show her wearing a false beard and a kilt, just like male kings did.

Which statue do you think makes Hatshepsut look more like a man?

HISTORY LINKS

NEFERTITI LIVED OVER A HUNDRED YEARS AFTER HATSHEPSUT AND WAS ONE OF THE MOST POWERFUL WOMEN IN THE HISTORY OF EGYPT. SHE WAS GIVEN THE TITLE 'CO-REGENT', WHICH MEANT SHE RULED ALONGSIDE HER HUSBAND, AKHENATON. TOGETHER THEY TRIED TO CHANGE EGYPT FOREVER. PEOPLE WERE MADE TO WORSHIP ONLY ONE GOD, ATEN. THIS THREW EGYPT INTO GREAT CONFUSION.

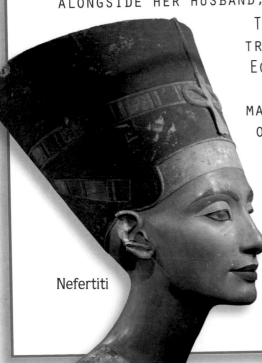

Nefertiti

A warrior king

We know about Hatshepsut because Hatshepsut wanted to show that she could do everything a male pharaoh could do and that meant going to war. Her Chief Treasurer wrote, 'I saw him (Hatshepsut) overthrowing the Nubian nomads, their chiefs brought before him (Hatshepsut) as prisoners.' Notice how Hatshepsut is referred to as 'him'.

HOW DO WE KNOW?

Hatshepsut probably didn't look exactly like the stone carvings of her because all pharaohs were portrayed like gods, without faults. But we can find out about Hatshepsut and her life from Egyptian writing and stone carvings.

Hieroglyphs

In ancient Egypt scribes wrote on papyrus. It is a natural material that decays, so very few documents have survived. However, Egyptians also painted scenes and hieroglyphs (see pages 18–19) on the walls of tombs, which were deep underground and usually blocked up so very little light could get to them. This meant they did not fade away.

You can still see the colours on this wall painting inside Hatshepsut's temple.

FASCINATING FACTS

WHY DO COLOURS FADE IN THE SUN? IMAGINE PAINTINGS, SUCH AS THE ONES ON THE WALLS OF HATSHEPSUT'S TEMPLE THAT ARE EXPOSED TO THE SUN. LIGHT IS MADE UP OF ALL THE COLOURS OF THE RAINBOW AND WHEN THEY FALL ON THE PAINTINGS THOSE COLOURS ARE ABSORBED INTO THEM. WHEN THAT HAPPENS THEY BEGIN TO BREAK DOWN THE DYES IN THE PAINT.

Stone carvings and statues

Stonemasons carved hieroglyphs and pictures into temple walls and on obelisks. These tell the stories of pharaohs down through the ages and since they were carved into stone they have survived to this day. We also have many statues of Hatshepsut. A careful study of each one reveals something different about her.

In some statues Hatshepsut has a beard to make her look like a man.

A defaced statue of Hatshepsut

Defaced images

After her death someone chipped away the face of Hatshepsut on many of her statues. Who might have ordered this destruction, and why? One suspect is her stepson, Thutmose III. He may have been resentful towards Hatshepsut for not allowing him to become ruler. The second suspect is Akhenaton. He defaced many statues when he became pharaoh to stop people worshipping any god other than Aten, the great creator god.

Bread

EVERYDAY LIFE

Most of what we know about ancient Egypt is about how pharaohs or other rich people lived but what about everyday life for everyone else?

Eating

Bread was the main source of food for Egyptians. They cooked flat bread flavoured with spices, garlic and herbs. Bread could also be sweetened with dates, figs and honey. Many kinds of fruit and vegetables were grown and beer was drunk by everyone as it was much safer than drinking water.

This model of a bakery was found in an Egyptian tomb.

FASCINATING FACTS

MOULDY BREAD WAS RUBBED ON SKIN TO HEAL INFECTED CUTS. EGYPTIANS DID NOT KNOW WHY IT WORKED BUT TODAY WE KNOW THAT SOME MOULDS CONTAIN A FUNGUS THAT ACTS AS AN **ANTIBIOTIC**. WE CALL IT PENICILLIN.

Relaxing

Senet was the most popular board game in ancient Egypt. Ka, the chief tomb builder around the time of Hatshepsut, said that his idea of a perfect afterlife was playing senet with his wife in their summerhouse.

Game board and counters for playing senet

Going to work

Hundreds of people were employed by Hatshepsut when she gave orders for temples and monuments to be built at Karnak in Thebes. There would have been stonemasons, artists, engineers, scribes and lots of **slaves** fetching, carrying, pulling, lifting, shoving and dragging building materials. Food grown by farmers and fish caught by local fishermen was transported by boat and cart for traders to sell in busy market places.

My own research

About fifty years after Hatshepsut died a scribe called Nakht built a tomb for himself and his wife, Tawy. Wall paintings inside his tomb show scenes from everyday life in ancient Egypt.

Look at the picture below of one of the wall paintings.
Can you see people cutting trees and sowing seeds?
What else are they doing?

HATSHEPSUT'S LEGACY

Hatshepsut was the most successful female pharaoh. How did she die and which of her achievements are worth remembering?

How did Hatshepsut die?

Poisoned by her stepson?

Some historians think Hatshepsut may have been poisoned by her stepson, Thutmose III, so he could become pharaoh. However it is more likely that Thutmose decided to wait for her to die from natural causes. He still had time on his side. In fact, Thutmose III went on to rule Egypt for 48 years.

Poisoned by skin cream?

Scientists at the University of Bonn in Germany have analysed the contents of a bottle that was part of Hatshepsut's possessions. The ancient ointment contains a highly poisonous ingredient that could have caused skin cancer. If that is true then Hatshepsut accidentally killed herself with a skin cream.

Rich Egyptian women used lots of make-up to make themselves beautiful but Hatshepsut's cream was probably used to treat eczema.

FASCINATING FACTS

EGYPTIAN MEN WORE MAKE-UP AS WELL AS WOMEN. RICH PEOPLE WERE MORE LIKELY TO WEAR BLACK EYE MAKE-UP, ROUGE ON CHEEKS AND LIPS AS WELL AS PERFUMED OILS THAT PROTECTED THE SKIN FROM THE SUN AND SAND.

Which mummy?

For years archaeologists were unsure which of several mummies was the body of Hatshepsut. But in 2007 they found a tooth in a box belonging to Hatshepsut. The tooth matched a hole in the mouth of one of the mummies. And when **DNA** samples from the mummy were compared with those of her relatives they got a match.

Most archaeologists agree that this is the body of Hatshepsut, but some are still not sure.

Reasons to remember Hatshepsut

1. Hatshepsut should be remembered as a very successful ruler of Egypt. Perhaps this was the reason why someone tried to erase all trace of her reign.

2. Hatshepsut made Egypt strong and wealthy by improving trade with other countries such as the land of Punt.

3. Hatshepsut built the magnificent mortuary temple at Deir el-Bahri which today remains one of the greatest buildings we have from ancient Egypt.

4. Hatshepsut promoted people like her advisor Senenmut because of their ability and not simply because they came from a rich family.

TIMELINE

3000 BCE

2750 BCE

2650 BCE
FIRST PYRAMID BUILT
FOR PHARAOH DJOSER

2500 BCE

3100 BCE
NARMER UNITES EGYPT AND
BECOMES THE FIRST PHARAOH

2560 BCE
GREAT PYRAMID
OF GIZA BUILT
FOR PHARAOH
KHUFU

2250 BCE

2055 BCE
WORK
BEGINS
ON THE
TEMPLE AT
KARNAK

1550 BCE
PHARAOH
AHMOSE I
DEFEATS THE
HYKSOS AND
RE-UNITES
ALL EGYPT

2000 BCE

1770 BCE
INVADERS
(HYKSOS)
FROM THE
MIDDLE
EAST RULE
ALL EGYPT

c.1483 BCE
HATSHEPSUT BEGINS WORK ON
HER MORTUARY TEMPLE AT
DEIR EL-BAHRI

c.1504 BCE
HATSHEPSUT IS
BORN

1750 BCE

c.1481 BCE
HATSHEPSUT
ORGANISED A TRADE
VISIT TO PUNT

1600 BCE

1555 BCE
BEGINNING OF
NEW KINGDOM, A
500-YEAR PERIOD
OF PEACE AND
PROSPERITY

1500 BCE

1479 BCE
HATSHEPSUT
BECOMES REGENT
QUEEN, RULING
IN PLACE OF
HER STEPSON

1539 BCE
PHARAOHS BEGIN TO
BUILD TOMBS IN THE
VALLEY OF THE KINGS

1458 BCE
HATSHEPSUT
DIES

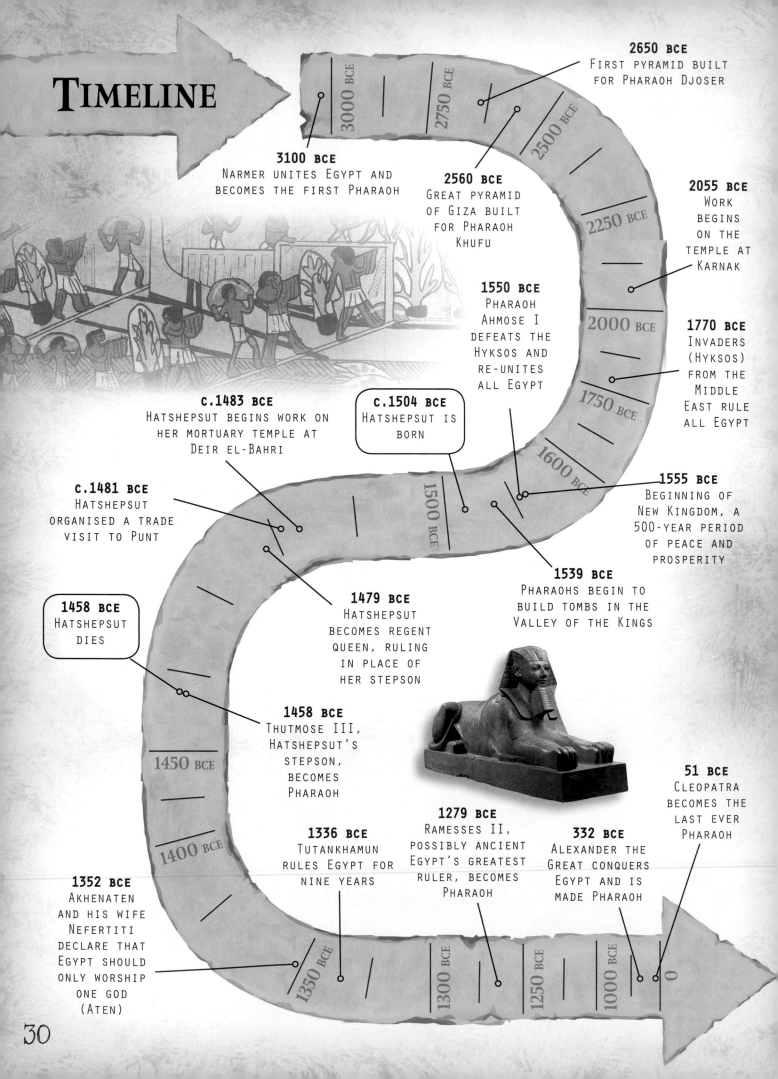

1458 BCE
THUTMOSE III,
HATSHEPSUT'S
STEPSON,
BECOMES
PHARAOH

51 BCE
CLEOPATRA
BECOMES THE
LAST EVER
PHARAOH

1450 BCE

1279 BCE
RAMESSES II,
POSSIBLY ANCIENT
EGYPT'S GREATEST
RULER, BECOMES
PHARAOH

332 BCE
ALEXANDER THE
GREAT CONQUERS
EGYPT AND IS
MADE PHARAOH

1336 BCE
TUTANKHAMUN
RULES EGYPT FOR
NINE YEARS

1400 BCE

1352 BCE
AKHENATEN
AND HIS WIFE
NEFERTITI
DECLARE THAT
EGYPT SHOULD
ONLY WORSHIP
ONE GOD
(ATEN)

1350 BCE

1300 BCE

1250 BCE

1000 BCE

0

GLOSSARY

Antibiotic a substance that can stop the growth of bacteria and cure infections

Canopic jars a container used by ancient Egyptians to store internal organs as part of the mummification process

Cartouche an oval shape which contains a set of ancient Egyptian hieroglyphs, often representing the name of a king or queen

DNA the chemical in the cells of animals and plants that carries genetic information

Dynasty a series of rulers of a country who all belong to the same family

Frankincense tree resin that is burnt to give a pleasant smell

Limestone a type of white stone

Mortuary temple a building constructed to commerate and worship an Egyptian pharaoh after their death

Mummification the process of preserving a body by treating it with special oils and wrapping it in cloth

Myrrh sticky tree resin that is used to make perfume and incense

Napoleon French military leader and emperor who lived from 1769–1821

Obelisk a tall stone column with four sides, put up in memory of an event or person

Pharaoh a ruler of ancient Egypt, who ruled as a god on Earth

Regent a person acting as ruler in place of the king who is too young or ill to rule

Seven Wonders of the World the seven most spectacular man-made structures of ancient times

Slaves people who are considered to be owned by others and are forced to work for no pay

Tomb a large grave, often built of stone, above or below the ground

THE GREAT HAPSHEPSUT QUIZ

1. What desert covers most of Egypt?

2. Who was the chief of all Egyptian gods?

3. Hatshepsut lived in the city of Thebes but what is it called today?

4. In which two countries does the River Nile have its source?

5. What was the most common drink in ancient Egypt and why?

6. What job did Hatshepsut's father have?

7. What name was given to the first pyramid ever built?

8. What city was the very first capital of Egypt?

9. What name was given to the great sun god?

10. During mummification, what body parts are placed in canopic jars?

11. How big were the boats that sailed to Punt?

12. What made the pyramids so bright when they were newly built?

Answers on page 32

INDEX

QUIZ ANSWERS

My own research, page 15: cow = Nekhbet, hippo = Taweret,
crocodile = Sobek, falcon = Horus

The Great Hatshepsut Quiz, page 31

1. Sahara **2.** Amun **3.** Luxor **4.** Uganda and Ethiopia **5.** Beer because it was safe to
drink **6.** He was a general in the Egyptian army **7.** The Step Pyramid **8.** Memphis
9. Ra **10.** Organs including the stomach, lungs and liver
11. 20 m long and 5 m wide **12.** Polished white limestone and gold decoration